The *Oldie*
BOOK OF CARTOONS

'Sorry – wrong planet'

.NAF.

'I love coming here for dinner parties – their
cheese board is out of this world!'

The Oldie
BOOK OF CARTOONS

Chosen by
David Abberton

This edition published by Oldie Publications Ltd in 2021

First published in 2018
by Oldie Publications Ltd

23 Great Titchfield Street, London W1W 7PA
www.theoldie.co.uk

ISBN 13 978-1-901170-32-0

A catalogue record for this book
is available from the British Library

Printed in the UK by St Ives Group

Introduction

The last few years have been sadly dominated by one thing – the pandemic. And there are some very funny cartoons about the dreaded virus in this marvellous new cartoon book, selected by David Abberton.

That's one of the magical things about cartoons. They can take the saddest things – like Covid-19 – and make light of them without leaving a bad taste in the mouth. Cartoonists aren't cancelled the way writers are. And that's because they are working on a different, comic plane, where nothing should ever be taken too seriously.

Take the cartoon on this book's cover by the terrific Nick Downes – one of those rare cartoonists who combine a gifted artist's line with a fine line in dark humour. If, in real life, a shrink had a patient who said, 'I especially liked the part where Bambi's mother got shot,' they'd be on the phone to the police in an instant.

But, in cartoon world, all that matters is that something is funny – and the darker the dark humour, the funnier the cartoon is.

Cartoons are little escapes – not just from the articles in *The Oldie*, which, brilliant as they are, take longer to read than a one-line caption. But they are also escapes from the world, a flight into fantasy: a world where dinosaurs talk, and cavemen have a sophisticated, modern take on Stone Age life.

Cartoons also have a language of their own. This book is full of our old friends: the two wise-cracking figures left on the desert island; the Grim Reaper popping up all over the place. Their familiarity means that, in order to get a laugh, they have to be funnier and funnier each time they appear. The desert island inhabitants and Grim Reapers are on better form than ever on these pages.

I've noticed a few new tropes emerging in the comforting fantasy world of cartoons in recent months (along with those pandemic gags). Galley slaves comparing notes while they row their boat are becoming increasingly popular; as is the gruesome bedtime story as told by an apparently wholesome mother. And there are many more surgeons being alarmingly blithe as they cut open another poor patient.

All dark scenes in real life; all irresistible here.

HARRY MOUNT,
Editor, *The Oldie*

'It says, "Go paperless! Opt to receive future messages by text, email... "'

'When you retire, will you be doing it from home?'

'A rare Picasso family photo'

'Tell me again, Dad, how you smote the auditors and drove the tax men into the wilderness'

'I can't wait to meet him. On his profile he said he was a Navy Seal'

'When the snow lay all about, deep and crisp and even...'

'If you don't mind my asking – why the black armband?'

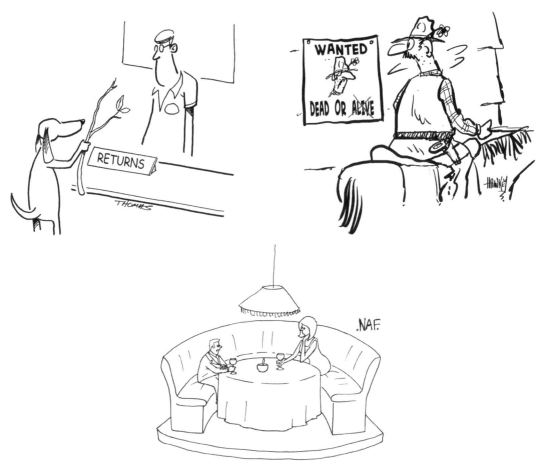

'No, not "stuntman"... "stunted" '

'The only room I have available, at the moment, is the "married, but sleeping in separate beds" suite'

'Delia says nothing about lizard's leg and owlet's wing'

'My, my, Grandma, what an unconventional lifestyle you have'

'I'm bipolar'

Hafeez.

HE'LL GROW INTO THEM

HE'LL GROW INTO THEM

THEN

NOW

'I'm starting to get a little worried about the company my Colin's been keeping lately'

TIME TRAVELLING SOCIETY

'Sorry I'm late... or early... or on time'

'I like you – you're different'

'And any improvements to the
building have been strictly cosmetic'

'Oh, I remember now – it's not the
food that's fabulous here; it's the prices'

'He's the last of the Mohicans'

'I really saved today! Everything was
25 per cent to 40 per cent off, and
our money was earning only 2 per
cent at the bank!'

'That funny sound you heard was
your warranty expiring'

If unicorns existed

'Maybe we should drive a stake through his heart, just to be sure?'

'Bill and I both hate the same books'

'How about cross-dress Thursdays'?

'Anything to declare?'

'Sometimes it's just nice to get out of the city'

'This is England. You didn't have a great fall. You had a great autumn!'

'My eyes are up here'

'Are they locally sourced?'

'I've done my 10,000 steps!'

'In a way, you can say that marriage is like binge dating'

'We hear you can make people disappear.'

'Gimme two fingers of
lapsang souchong...'

GUILT TRIP

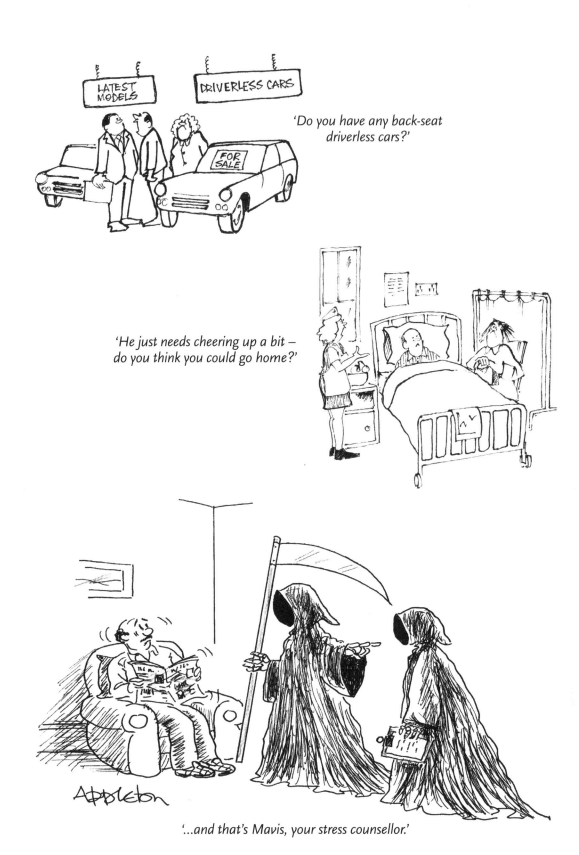

'Do you have any back-seat driverless cars?'

'He just needs cheering up a bit – do you think you could go home?'

'...and that's Mavis, your stress counsellor.'

'You can be anything you want to be, Timmy: a doctor, a lawyer, a stockbroker...'

'I can call a solicitor what?'

"INHERITED PIECES OF EIGHT"

Long John Silver Spoon

K.J.Lamb

McGeaiy

Kipper Williams

'Daddy, which relative's history did YOU investigate for a television documentary about what they did in the Great War?'

Nick Downs

'He turned out to be a sugarless daddy'

'You ever step on one of those things? Youch – it hurts!'

WHY DO WE STILL HAVE A LANDLINE?

TO FIND MY MOBILE

'I'll take the non-vegan option'

k.J.Lamb

'I wandered lonely as a cloud,
when all at once I saw...'

'I wish I'd brought a book or something'

'My compliments to the microwave-operator'

'Now then ... what was it I came up here for?'

'OK – what shall we not talk about?'

'Narcissus feels outnumbered'

'You all know General Intelligence from I.T.'

'What's your problem? I got you a Margherita and I got myself a Hawaiian'

'What rotten luck'

'I bet Greta eats
her broccoli'

'Why don't we just sell our horns and move to Florida?'

'Can't you show some self-reliance for once?'

'We must be entering Japanese waters'

'Has this rhubarb been forced?'

'Every once in a while, my wife agrees
with me, just to keep me off balance'

'A fine choice, madam'

'Ever get one of those days when
nothing anyone says offends you?'

'Imagine you're interviewing for a job,
and the interviewer asks you a series of
asinine hypothetical questions.
How would you react?'

'When he said he had commissioned a statue of his one true love,
I thought he meant me'

'I dunno – we don't know where he's been'

NickDowmes

'Thank you for confessing. Your confession is important to us but, owing to the present situation, all lines are currently engaged'

'It's not a jungle out there'

'I don't know, Rembrandt.
You and your selfies!'

'Oh no – Easter-egg hunt saboteurs'

'What are you waiting for, Harry?'

'What the hell's a great crested newt!?!'

'Oh, all right ... could you *mime* exactly what happened on the night in question?'

'We find the "naughty roof"' more
effective than the "naughty step"'

'I'd say it's athlete's foot'

'It's called "Dinner" and it was painted just after his marriage break-up'

'Do you know who I was?'

'His lordship goes for a run every morning'

SNOW WHITE AND THE 7 OLD DWARFS...

GRUMPY GRUMPY GRUMPY GRUMPY GRUMPY GRUMPY GRUMPY

PAUL WOOL

THE ANGEL OF THE LORD HAS JUST ADDED TO THEIR INSTAGRAM CHRISTMAS STORY

K.J.Lamb

SOUP KITCHEN

NOT YOU AGAIN?

ROBERT THOMPSON

'Isn't it a bit early for Christmas tat?'

'I clapped between movements
at a symphony'

'I hear she's started burlesque classes'

'This is great, Angela ... just lose these, move those, change that, that, that, that and that... Then start again'

'Do something to amuse the children, Albert. Invent Christmas'

'Help yourself to anything in the fridge'

'If only they knew half of what we get up to...'

'So it's true, then – you and Brian have split up'

'Keep them coming'

'If I appear overqualified, I can tone
down the exaggerations'

'I'm looking for an
"I told you so" card for
my husband'

'Derivative or what?!'

'I was just wondering if I could get some time off to hibernate this winter...'

'I forgot – which colour bin do plastics go in?'

'How thoughtful: "Best Wife in the 0.0000007 Per Cent of the World I'm Personally Acquainted With"'

'I'm sorry. I'm just looking for something less complicated'

'There's always one misery guts'

'If you let him back in just once, he'll want to sleep with us every night'

'Yes, it is a very stressful time of year'

'I had ants for lunch. Do you have any zucchini?'

'I dunno – what do you wanna do?'

'He didn't wake up this morning'

'Are you going to eat that?'

'Bloody women drivers!'

'It's amazing, really –
married for 50 years and
died minutes apart'

'Where would you
like to not be able to
afford to go on holiday
this year?'

GRILLED, SOUTHERN FRIED, CURRIED OR CRISPY?

'Isn't it great? I found a little "Classroom Mode" switch behind their ears'

'That boy's really destined for something'

'999? My husband's unresponsive'

'If a standard-capacity magazine holds 30 rounds and the shooter fires off 16, how many bullets are left in the gun?'

'I just met their leader. Quick – let's get out of here!'

'And then what happened?'

'Give us a few days and we'll call to tell you we've given the job to someone else'

IF SHAKESPEARE WERE ALIVE TODAY

'So in this one we find out that Hamlet, who didn't actually die in the last movie, became an evil wizard and faces off against Ophelia's son and they have a big fight and then Hamlet says, "I am your father!"'

'How long have you suspected you're being followed?'

'Indoor voice, sweetie – use your
indoor voice'

'Come on, chaps – a few more feet to go and we'll be the first men to
conquer the awesome J2 mountain'

'Are you sure we're not coming up to a waterfall?'

'Such a lovely day – he's outside
playing in the garden'

'Our apologies.
This is our
oldest wine!'

'Are we still middle-class?'

'Let's face it, Gabriel – heaven's not what it was'

'I've found people are generally good and will do just about anything to make you happy'

'When all at once – I failed to see'

'Help me gather driftwood – together
with these palm fronds, we can fashion
a crude puppet theatre'

'Jenkins, did we get that new 3-D copier yet?'

'It turns out you're not A, B or AB but the much rarer ABBA blood group'

'I'm not really a cat or a dog person'

'Let's go someplace where we can text'

'You can't switch it off'

'Sorry – wrong house'

'You've been lying on that thing ever since you invented it'

'Don't look now, but those awful bores the Johnsons are waving at us'

'One day, son, all this will be yurts!'

2020
GLASTONBURY
FESTIVAL
Cancelled

'For our next number, you'll be getting a zesty hint of Cole Porter, with the sumptuous essence of Prokofiev, underpinned by the delicate and persistent, velvety notes of Scott Joplin and Mozart with the well-rounded and refreshing finish of Purcell and the bright, crisp tones of Wagner'

'Can you shift, Dad?
I'm building the
Ashford Lorry Park'

ARE WE
THERE YET?

'The reward used to be food. Now it's
Facebook access for ten minutes'

'On the other
hand, it's always
people season'

'Quick – lock the doors'

'And now I'd like you to give a warm welcome to our latest superhero – Manman'

'No, that's also a surveillance satellite'

'Rodin's The Whatever'

'I wish someone would hurry up and invent "the spare"...'

'I'd forgotten it was "take your
daughter to work day" today'

'Maybe it's more productive to tell me
what you're not anxious about these days'

'Here's my card – please
don't ever call me'

'Yes, of course I will, Gerry, and I've got something for you, too'

'You're lucky it's just lions. Last week some poor bastard was savaged by the media'

'Put your finger here, nurse'

'It's been months now, Edna, but I still can't see any improvement. I'm just worried you might not be getting anything at all out of this class'

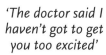

'And the airlines refunded everyone in full'

'Me?! Raid your drinks cabinet, Doctor Jekyll?!'

'The doctor said I haven't got to get you too excited'

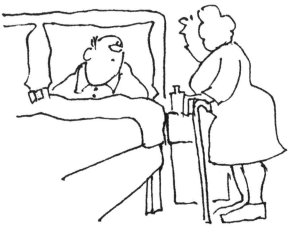

'Before we leave, remember to put on your afterlife jackets'

'Don't worry – it's medical marijuana'

'It's one of those impossible-to-put-down beach reads'

'Everything all right with the photo of your meal, sir?'

'Hi honey, I'm home workplace hybrid!'

'125 is the new 100'

'Oh, we only have tofu down here'

'So, if we're anti-Christ, does that mean we're pro-science?'

YOUR
DINNER
IS ON
PAGE 21

COOKERY
FOR
BEGINNERS

BED
WORLD

'Well, how are we supposed to know if
it's the right bed for us?'

'It's not very easy being a living deadly sin'

'For my next trick, I will save for a mortgage deposit – while renting!'

'The locals are a bit stand-offish at first. But once they get to know you, they become deeply unpleasant'

'If you use the wrong trans pronoun,
I'll call the police!'

'We're a little concerned. Usually by
now, they've taken their first selfie'

'All I said was "Your round"'

'You could have told me I've been talking to
your bottom for fifteen minutes'

Navied

'We see this as a win-win-lose situation'   PHiL WiTTe

'What's happened to you?
You used to be so young'

'Aw, come on –
before they ban it'

'Well, yes, I'm happy – but I feel I could be happier'

'You couldn't have
brought two chargers?'

Naviet

'I don't want to live on the edge but I
wouldn't mind visiting it'

'Let me guess – another
cartoon that reminds you of us'

'We'll get an ambulance to you just as soon as we can raise a television crew'

'We're looking for applicants who are accident-prone'

'It's haunted by an 18th-century farmer who can't believe what we paid for it'

NICK DOWNES

'Come and meet Marjorie – she's a scream!'

K.J.Lamb

'Whatever you do, don't take me to your leader'

STONEHENGE - THE EARLY DAYS

'Well, that's the scaffolding done – what's next?'

'It's been taken care of'

NICK DOWNES

'We are doing the
Great Battles – Alcohol
Addiction, Self-Harm,
Drug Abuse, Demons,
Obesity...'

'Who the hell is Joe?'

'I think I see your problem'

'The shareholders want one of us to self-identify as a female'

'I never knew there was a written exam as well'

'Good evening. I'm Ed and
I'll be waiting for your table'

GRETA GARBO'S GARDEN SHED.

I WANT
TO BE
A LAWN.

GRASS
SEED

DECEPTION

'He's at a meeting'

'You're not the
man of my
dreams, but you
have been known
to put me to sleep'

'You think you
got a raw deal
– I was damned
with faint praise'

'He was about
this tall, my
weight
and colour'

'No, Joe! Not through there – it's a trompe l'oeil...!'

'Stand back or I shout'

'I'm afraid it's curiosity'"

'Well at least he's not sitting at home
scrounging off the government, darling'

'It's getting more and more difficult
to be smug middle-class'

'When the music
stops, sit down in the
nearest chair.
Whoever doesn't get
a chair will be made
redundant'

'Take a letter, Brother Francis – "Dear Father Sebastian..."'

'We all draw on our walls but he has to make such a big deal of it!'

'Oh for goodness' sake!
Stop celebrating Britishness...'

'Good book?'

'So you're a
cartoonist too?'

'A great man – but
terribly scared of heights'

BUT MOST
OF ALL,
YOU'VE LET
YOURSELF
DOWN

'Frankie, you're not
supposed to see me on
our wedding day!'

ROBERT THOMPSON

'Must do Munch'

'The double deluxe gets both of you upstairs
before you can forget why you're going'

'One day, son, all this will be going with me'

'I'm very pleased with Fred's hip replacement'

'Strange that you happened to invent the wheel just before my mother visits'

'It's been a bit draughty since he sold one of his pictures'

95

'Nice guy but a bit too deep for me'

'Hi – it's me. I'm on the train'

'Is it my back hair?'

'He says he thought he might as well make himself useful while he was waiting for you'

'As you can see, folks, there was once a strong English influence here on Easter Island'

'Hello. My name is Malcolm and I have imaginary friends'

'You said it again – "My smother" '

The Junior Mafia

JAMIE OLIVER TWIST

'What's mansplaining? It's when one explains to someone, typically a woman, in a manner regarded as condescending or patronizing, that one is actually bull-shitting'

'Actually, I don't think it is a Lowry...'

'Shouldn't he have reached that age where he can't _stand_ to be in the same room as us by now?'

'Are the calamari fresh?'

'You can't tell me she hasn't
had work done'

'I'm getting a noise checked out up the
street, but I'll give you £50 for some
car jargon I can throw around'

'Fantastic, I've finally solved
my weight problem'

'So, to sum up...'

'Kids nowadays
are too fat and
lazy to walk.
I have to deliver'

'I walk into their
yard every few
days and knock
over their trash.
How do you know
the Johnsons?'

Ken Pyne

'It's so good to get out to the shops again'

'You would tell me if you weren't happy, wouldn't you?'

'At this time, if everyone would please switch their palates to airplane mode'

'Sorry, but I've completely forgotten what I came up here for'

'The Kitchen Islands dead ahead, Cap'n!'

'An elephant got into the room!'

'Well, if you think the Tiger Room is impressive, wait until you see the Ex-Wife Room'

'Honestly, Harold. You're 40 years old and you still can't hibernate without a bed-time story!'

'It's always the "Good Book" –
never the "Great Book"'

'One thing about Mondrian –
you always know where you are
with him'

'I'm not driving, sir –
I'm just here to give
you my opinions on
topical issues'

'Now I wish I hadn't ordered all those appetisers'

'The nurse will be giving you a self-testing kit for your halitosis, Mr Gurble'

LAZY BLUES MAN

'Be honest. Does my bum look big in this?'

'Here come the Atoms.
Don't believe a word they say.
They make up everything'

'He's been unbearable since that artist painted him...'

'Do you know what gender he will be when he leaves school?'

'What are you staring at? Haven't you seen a 4x4 before?'

'It's still a mystery why they get drawn to the beach'

'Is the only exit through the gift shop?'

Dandruff shaker

'Of course I didn't marry James just for his money. I married him for his shares, his property and his money '

'He always had green fingers'

'Mind if I use your toilet?'

'British'

K.J.Lamb

'Your son's fooling around has
reached intolerable levels.'

'I've already had one for the road – so let's have
another in case there's an unexpected detour'

'Simon has a wonderful nose for wine'

'Gold, frankincense and myrrh?
Sorry – no trade agreement...'

'So, basically, Marvin, never give up on your dreams'

'Actually, I think I'll walk '

'Sorry. I don't do Brexit'

*'Just look at the poor things...
Same routine day in, day out...'*

'Run along and press play'

'Is there a <u>Mrs</u> Mutant Space Creature?'

'Nightshift is always livelier at Halloween'

'This is an upwardly mobile phone, sir. It converts everything you say into the Queen's English'

'Santa's little self-helper'

' Look everyone! A water vole!'

'...Dear Sir,...'

'What, no film crew?'

'No, Harold. Not badgers'

'They suspect arson'

'I didn't think our divorce would be so amicable that you'd still be here'

'We met on 'Blind Date'!'

'Did you have to pay for excess baggage, too?'

'Hello – Carter's Corporate Cake Company? This cake you've supplied – just how old is it?'

'When did you first start feeling grim?'

'Shhh – keep quiet. If he manages to get it, he'll be doing the whole world a favour'

'The four-course men of the apocalypse'

'He misses the Cones Hotline more than he'll admit'

'Could you make it a little longer?'

'Moses – how many
times must I tell you?
Stop playing with
your soup!'

'He wants to see his money before he goes...'

'Well, you have a word with him about queue-jumping'

'...and this is Sylvia and me, going through a bad patch...'

'And it all ends up being
stored in the cloud'

'He claims he was at a fancy dress
party and there's been some mistake.
What should I do?'

'I told you we were over-dressed'

'How would you feel about being
thrown in at the deep end'

'An obscene amount of money
for your thoughts'

'Maureen and I are going through a bit of a rough patch!'

'Miss Thompson – take a suicide note'

'On second thoughts, I will
have the garlic bread'

'What upsets me, Daddy, is that
everyone knew it was going to happen'

'We've put your husband into a medically induced coma, because he is _such_ a whiner'

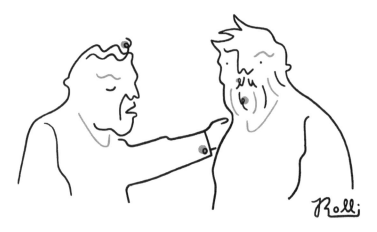

'Anyway, it was nice talking and talking while you stood there in agony waiting for the opportunity to say even one more word'

'Could you write, 'I promise this is my last novel'?'

'I have a fear of abandonment...'

'We're living the life we want, as long as we don't want much'

'And I'm doing that bloody online assertiveness-training course – OK?'

'My art speaks for itself'

'I'm in for identity fraud'

'It's long and wooden and got a sharp,
pointy, metal bit at the end'

'What about taxing the rich and giving the poor free healthcare and education?'

'Do you have to keep checking your messages?'

'How about this line?'

'Now I understand'

'It's so wonderful you're buying me an engagement ring. But why do we need a getaway driver?'

'Whoa, volcanic glass? VERY high-tech'

'Have you tried turning it off and on again?'

'I just want my boy to take an active hand in the business if he wants to take over when I retire'

'The granny annexe was the
wife's idea!'

'You're under a lot of pressure. Think about all the expectations
people have when your name starts with 'Great''

'We're in the wrong cartoon, aren't we?'

'NASA's first photo of the landing to find life on Mars'

'You should have come to see me sooner'

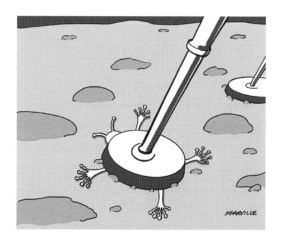

'Do you, Narcissus, take ... er...'

'How about a bit of role-play to spice things up? We could pretend we don't hate each other'

'I couldn't find a nailfile – so I brought you some nail polish and lip gloss...'

'He just lives in the past'

'Got any red tape?'

'He says you'll like his friend — he says he's a well-known film actor and you'll recognise him when you see him'

'Carrie, are you wearing my trousers?'

'For God's sake, let me get drunk first!'

' "Found him?" – but I've rented out his room'

'How quintessentially English – maiden
aunts e-scootering to evensong'

'He was a great actor'

'I'll double what she's paying, if you say
you can't find me'

A MAN DOESN'T WALK INTO A PUB...

PANDEMIC COMEDY

IAN BAKER.

DISCIPLINARY ACTION MAN

" I SHOULD NOT HAVE SAID/DONE THAT... I DEEPLY REGRET..."

K.J.Lamb

THE STYX

KenPyne

'Well, we did hope we could go on a cruise this year'

'It belonged to my ex ... it's the closest he came to high fidelity'

'It was your idea to domesticate it – you walk it!'

'When I say I lost my wife, I mean in a poker game'

'I learned that I'm one of those people
you can fool all of the time'

'The sensor on the back makes a noise
if you park too close to something'

'A very mild form of Tourette's,
you say? You cad!'

'I think it would be better
on the other wall'

WITHDRAWALS

'You need hold-ups'

'He's started rehearsing his pointless coughing'

'Fine! You plan the next holiday'

'It feels more like living at work
than working from home'

'You'd touch me more if I were a screen'

'Remember – no snacking
between snacks'

'To be honest, usually both
members of the couple are alive'

'I was getting bored with sitting around
at home doing nothing – so that's why I
decided to take up meditation'

'I realise the lads have got to celebrate after winning, but not on the tapestry'

'When you said you were taking me to your yacht for lunch I imagined something different entirely'

'He just discovered his reflection'

BRITISH
FASHION
COUNCIL

SO IN   SO OUT

K.J.Lamb

'One day, son, all this will be
your brother's'

'The gentleman who thinks he's a gecko is waiting for
you in the consulting room'

' I wish you'd come to me earlier about your son's head lice, Mrs Cloke'

'I've invented this thing called the dog kennel —
all we have to do now is domesticate a wolf'

'Cream first, _then_ jam'

'But is it a _happy_ sham marriage?'

' He's a vegetarian'

Glossary of cartoonists

Ace
AJ Smith
Andrew Birch
Andy McKay (NAF)
Appleton
B E Dawson
Bill Abbott
Bill Huball
Bill Proud (BP)
Bill Round
Bill Stott
Bob Eckstein (bob)
Carol Stokes
Catherine Phillips (Grizelda)
Cisner
Clive Collins
Cluff
Colin Wheeler
Colin Whittock
Crowden Satz (SATZ)
Dan McConnell
Darling
Dave Parker
David Austin
De la Nougererde
Drew Panckeri
Ed McLachlan
Fran
Fransan
Ged Melling (GED)
Geoff Thompson
Geoff Waterhouse
GF
Gordon Gurvan (GG)
GPR
Grain
Gray Joliffe (Gray)
Ham Khan (Ham)

Holland
Martin Honeysett
Howard
Hunger
Huw Aaron
Inés
Inglis Thorurn (Inglis)
Ivor Healy (Ivor)
J Di Chiarro
Jelli Benn
John Docherty (Jorodo)
John Lightbourne
Jones
Julian Mosedale (JM)
Kathryn Lamb
Ken Pyne
Kieran Meehan
Lawly
Len
Paul Lowe
Mark Lewis
Meyrick Jones
Michel Cambon
Michael Corrigan (Mico)
Mike Turner
Mike Williams
Neil Bennett (NB)
Neil Dishington (Dish)
Nick Downes
Nik Scott
Norman Jung
Peter King (Pak)
Pals
Pat Campbell
Paul Kales
Paul Lowe (Lowe)
Paul Shadbolt
Paul Wood

Paulson
Philip Berkin
Phil Witte
Prock
R Lowe
Rains
Red
Rigby
Rob Murray
Robert Thompson
Roger Latham
Rolli Writes
Ron Morgan
Ronan Lefebvre (Sti)
Roy Jones
Roy Nixon
Royston Robertson (Royston)
Rupert Besley
Sally Artz
Samson
Sewell
Simon Pearsall
Stephen Hutchinson (Bernie)
Steven Jones (Jonesy)
Stewart
Term Larson
Terry Carter
Terry Mazurke
Theo
Tom Kleh
Tony Eden
Tony Husband
Waldorf
Warner
Wilbur Dawbarn (Wilbur)
Wilson
Wren
Woodcock